Hale and Bopp
Two Guys Make History

by John David
illustrated by Dave Blanchette

Printed in the United States of America

ISBN 0-15-317321-1 – Hale and Bopp

Ordering Options
ISBN 0-15-318664-X (Package of 5)
ISBN 0-15-316987-7 (Grade 3 Package)

3 4 5 6 7 8 9 10 179 02 01 00

From the time he was three years old,
Thomas Bopp has loved watching the night sky.
He has made it his hobby.

On July 23, 1995, in Arizona, Bopp's hobby
brought him fame. He was looking at the night
sky through his telescope. He saw a faint glow he
had never seen before. He asked a friend who was
with him to check the star charts. These charts list
every known object in space. The glow was not on
the chart!

"Tom," his friend told him excitedly, "I think
you may have something!"

On that same night, in New Mexico, Alan Hale was out in his yard. He was also looking at the night sky through his telescope, as he often did.

It was a very clear night. Hale looked at a part of the sky he had been studying a few weeks earlier. Suddenly, he gasped in surprise.

Something new was there. It was a faint glow. Excited, Hale made a quick sketch of what he saw. As he went into the house, he looked back. The glow was still there.

Hale, too, checked his star charts. Like Bopp, he did not find the object on them. Quickly, Hale sent a message to a place in Massachusetts where all comets are tracked. He told the people at this center what he had seen.

Thomas Bopp also left messages with the center. The next morning, he got a message back. It said, "Congratulations, Tom. I believe you've discovered a new comet."

"That was one of the most exciting moments of my life!" Bopp said. Twelve hours after Hale and Bopp had first seen the comet, it had a name—Comet Hale-Bopp.

4

People everywhere heard about the comet. They started tracking it. They found out that Comet Hale-Bopp would come close to Earth in 1997.

People were expecting to see an amazing show when the comet arrived. It might even be the brightest comet in 400 years!

Some people were thrilled. Other people started to worry. Would the comet hit Earth? Other people wondered, "What is a comet, anyway?"

A comet is one kind of space object that orbits
the sun. The center of a comet is called its
nucleus. The nucleus is made up of particles of
ice, dust, and rock.

When a comet is far away from the sun, the
nucleus is a dark, frozen ball. As the comet comes
closer, it reflects the sun's light. The sun's energy
causes many changes in the comet.

The sun's warmth turns some of the ice in the nucleus into gas. This gas surrounds the comet and streams out behind it as a long tail. Some comets form only one tail, but most form two.

A gas tail can be millions of miles long. It is formed when the comet's gases come in contact with solar wind. Solar wind is a force that comes from the surface of the sun.

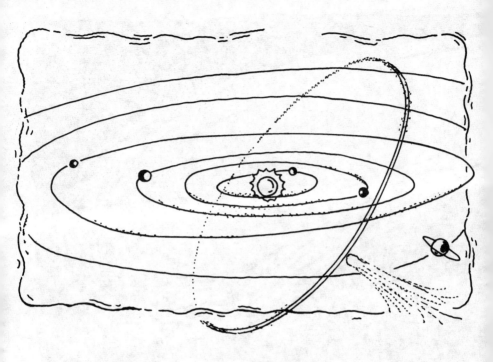

The gases in the tail soak up the sun's force or energy. They begin to glow with a fluorescent blue color. However, the fluorescent blue color is hard for people to see in the night sky. The gas tail may not look very bright.

Another kind of tail is made up of particles of dust from the comet. A dust tail is shorter and brighter than a gas tail.

The comet's orbit loops around the sun. As
the comet heads toward the sun, it passes Earth.

Some people worried that Comet Hale-Bopp
would hit Earth, but there was never any chance
of that. The closest it came was still 122 million
miles away.

In 1996, people became very excited. They
knew Comet Hale-Bopp would eventually be
bright enough to see without a telescope.

Comet Hale-Bopp was even more exciting than people had hoped. In early 1997, it could be seen in the sky every night. It was brightest in the middle of March. Except for the moon, Comet Hale-Bopp was the brightest object in the sky. Its tail, which was several million miles long, trailed off into the darkness.

In May 1997, the remarkable Comet Hale-Bopp had started to fade. By June, it could no longer be seen from the United States. By July, it was too far away to be seen from any part of Earth.

However, the comet still loops in orbit around the sun. The next time Comet Hale-Bopp will pass near Earth will be in the year 4377. So if you missed it this time, you really missed it! Meanwhile, Alan Hale and Thomas Bopp still study the night skies.

The sky is filled with billions of amazing objects. Many of them are still waiting to be discovered!

Solve This Puzzle

On graph paper, copy this crossword puzzle grid. Then fill it in with words from the story. (Turn the page to find the answers.)

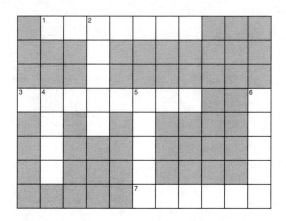

ACROSS

1. A comet's center
3. Comet ____-____
7. Bopp's first name

DOWN

2. An icy ball that orbits the sun
4. Hale's first name
5. A comet's path around the sun
6. These shine at night.

TAKE-HOME BOOK
Journeys of Wonder
Use with "Visitors from Space."

Answer:

	N	U	C	L	E	U	S			
			O							
			M							
H	A	L	E	B	O	P	P			S
	L		T		R					T
	A				B					A
	N				I					R
				T	H	O	M	A	S	